IMAGES
of America

WORLD WAR II
IN
TAMPA BAY

IMAGES
of America

WORLD WAR II
IN
TAMPA BAY

Alejandro M. de Quesada

ARCADIA

First published 1997
Copyright © Alejandro M. de Quesada, 1997

ISBN 0-7524-0888-7

Published by Arcadia Publishing,
an imprint of the Chalford Publishing Corporation,
One Washington Center, Dover, New Hampshire 03820.
Printed in Great Britain

Library of Congress Cataloging-in-Publication Data applied for

*To all the Floridians who served in the armed services during World War II.
Of the 250,000 who went to war, 5,848 never came home.*

Tampa's Grand Central Avenue is shown as it looked in 1942. (Courtesy Special Collections, University of South Florida.)

Contents

Acknowledgments

I would like to thank the following individuals and institutions who made this book possible: Vincent Luisi (director, Dunedin Historical Museum), Paul Eugen Camp (Special Collections, University of South Florida), Hal Hubener (Special Collections, Lakeland Public Library), John Lindstrom (St. Petersburg Historical Museum), Terry Dryman, and National Archives.

Introduction

This is a history, told in photographs, of the unified defense of the United States during World War II by the men and women who made the Tampa Bay region their home. The preparation of war brought new life into the Tampa area, a small town that was once the focus of the nation's attention when "Teddy" Roosevelt rode in with his Rough Riders in that "Splendid Little War" with Spain nearly forty-five years previous. Construction of MacDill Army Airfield, the oldest of the military airfields in the area, began in 1939. The site was picked due to the large size of the city of Tampa where it could easily accommodate personnel and their families with housing, schools, and other recreational facilities. The base was to be named in honor of Colonel Leslie MacDill, who was killed in a plane crash in 1938. At the same time that construction began on what was to become MacDill, the City of Tampa leased Drew Field to the Army for twenty-five years. On March 11, 1941, the first troops to arrive at the new airfield were members of a detachment of the 27th Air Base Squadron from Barksdale Field. A series of base commanders existed prior to the arrival of Colonel Clarence Tinker, who was promoted as commander of the 29th Bombardment Group at Drew Field and who landed the first plane on MacDill Field on January 17, 1941. As commander of the new MacDill Army Air Field, Tinker dedicated the runways in a public ceremony on April 14, 1941.

The outbreak of World War II saw the overnight existence of military airfields across the state of Florida. Tampa Bay became the main focal point in the state for training fighter and bombardier pilots. More than seven military airfields were located in the bay area, with Benjamin Field (site of Fort Homer Hesterly National Guard Armory) becoming the headquarters for the Third Army Air Force. Of these, the biggest of the military installations were Drew and MacDill Fields (both were built prior to the Japanese surprise attack on the U.S. Naval Fleet in Pearl Harbor, Hawaii). The need for more airfields forced the military to convert many county airports into functioning military facilities.

The war brought new life into the Tampa Bay area. St. Petersburg had suffered heavily with the bust of land speculation in the 1920s, and its tourist industry was on the decline. After the Japanese attack on Pearl Harbor and the declaration of war by the United States, the Tampa Bay area was "invaded" by thousands of military personnel from all branches of the military. As if by overnight, every hotel and apartment building in St. Petersburg was taken by the military for use as barracks for its men. The Don Cesar building was purchased by the army for use as a military hospital (During the war years, the Don Cesar would be known as Flak Hotel). The army then moved downward into Pass-A-Grille, a sleepy little community south of the Don Cesar.

Pinellas County began constructing an airport on the west shoreline of Tampa Bay in March 1941 on a 939-acre tract of county land. After Pearl Harbor, the airport was used as an Army Air Force military base and therefore named Pinellas Army Air Field. The 304th and 440th Fighter Squadrons based P-40s and, later, P-51s here for the duration of World War II. Both units were part of the 337th Fighter Group of the Third Army Air Force and served as combat training squadrons. Today, the old army airfield has become the St. Petersburg-Clearwater International Airport, which has expanded into a 2,000-acre complex and is home to one of the busiest Coast Guard Air Stations in the country.

In 1942, elements of the 252nd Coast Artillery took possession of the southern tip of the Pass-A-Grille Island from Third Avenue down to the tip where Pass-A-Grille Pass leads into the intercoastal waterways of the Gulf Coast beaches and Tampa Bay. The army relocated most of the residents out of the newly designated military installation with the exception of Mrs. Thomas Watson, the eighty-five-year-old widow of the co-inventor of the telephone. The top brass decided to string barbed wire around the house, making it a civilian enclave bordered on three sides by a military installation. A detachment of military police encamped on the nearby beach.

At the beginning of 1940, there were eight military installations in Florida. By 1943 there were one hundred seventy-two installations. The sheer magnitude of this nation's military might in the Tampa Bay area during the Second World War was so extensive that is nearly impossible to discuss all the installations which were scattered throughout the bay area in this short introduction. However, throughout this work, places will be mentioned such as Drew Army Air Field (AAFld) (Tampa), Henderson AAFld (Tampa), Page AAFld (Ft. Myers), Drane Army Air Field (Lakeland), Buckingham AAFld (Ft. Myers), Punta Gorda AAFld (Punta Gorda), Boca Chica AAFld (Boca Chica), Sarasota AAFld (Sarasota), Zephyrhills AAFld (Zephyrhills), and Bayboro CGAS (St. Petersburg).

The Tampa Bay area can serve as a representation of many other communities in the United States which were caught up in a time when the heat of a worldwide war came to our country's shores, when it was possible to have an enemy lurking behind from anywhere. As the military made its impact in the area, the civilians did their part for the war effort. On the homefront, women went to war brandishing hard hats and other tools of various trades that formerly were limited to men. Children and elderly men did their part in the war effort as well. German and Italian POWs soon began calling Tampa home with the establishment of nearby military installations. From shipbuilding to creating "Victory Gardens," civilian wartime deeds will not be forgotten. This is the story of these men and women, both military and civilian, and the significant roles they played during World War II in Tampa Bay.

One
Pre-War Tampa Bay

Taken in 1940, this peaceful image shows Tampa's skyline before war clouds hovered over the sleepy Southern town. (Courtesy Tampa-Hillsborough County Public Library System.)

A detachment of the Civilian Conservation Corps (CCC) marches past the St. Petersburg Colosseum. The CCC was a peacetime organization created by President Roosevelt as a way to provide employment during the economic depression of the 1930s. With military-style structure and training, the CCC made it an easy transition for members to join the armed forces when war broke out. (Courtesy A.M. de Quesada.)

Here we can see the Million Dollar Pier and a peaceful St. Petersburg skyline as it appeared in 1933. Note the Coast Guard vessels moored alongside the structure. In 1927 the Coast Guard opened a facility at nearby Bayboro Harbor. (Courtesy St. Petersburg Historical Society.)

Albert Whitted Airport shared its runways with the United States Coast Guard Station at Bayboro Harbor, c. 1940. (Courtesy St. Petersburg Historical Society.)

Across from the Coast Guard station is the United States Maritime Service Training Station. The Coast Guard established the installation in 1939 to train merchant seamen. As the installation grew with the outbreak of war, it was transferred to the U.S.M.S. in 1943. Note the training ships *Joseph Conrad* (center) and *American Seaman* (right). (Courtesy St. Petersburg Historical Society.)

A class photograph, taken on November 25, 1939, shows one of the very first classes of trainees to be trained by the Coast Guard. This image was taken aboard the *American Seaman*, a

training ship used by the recruits. (Courtesy St. Petersburg Historical Society.)

Fort DeSoto on Mullet Key is shown as it appeared during the 1940s. This fortification, built immediately after the Spanish-American War, was once a formidable harbor defense. Abandoned in the 1920s, this fort and its companion, Fort Dade on Egmont Key, were quickly taken over by the army when war broke out after Pearl Harbor. Mullet Key served as a bombing range and as a emergency landing for MacDill's bombers. (Courtesy St. Petersburg Historical Society.)

Two

The Army Air Corps
Comes to Town

93—U. S. Bombers from Mac Dill Field Army Base over Lafayette Street Bridge, Tampa, Fla.

A pre-war image shows U.S. bombers from MacDill Army Air Base over the bridge of Lafayette Street, presently Kennedy Boulevard. (Courtesy of A.M. de Quesada.)

This is Drew Field as it appeared in 1940, when it was transferred to the army. The City of Tampa leased the field to the army for twenty-five years at a cost of $1 per year. (Courtesy A.M. de Quesada)

The army quickly turned Drew Field into a military facility with the addition of barracks, warehouses, and improved runways. This photograph was taken from the "Base Photographic Laboratory, MacDill Field, Fla." (Courtesy Special Collections, University of South Florida.)

The barracks at Drew Army Air Field were home to many men during the war years. (Courtesy Special Collections, University of South Florida.)

This view shows one of the hangars being constructed at MacDill. The photograph was dated April 29, 1941. (Courtesy Special Collections, University of South Florida.)

Construction crews work on one of the hangars at MacDill in June 1941. Note the already constructed watertower in the distance behind the hangar. (Courtesy Tampa-Hillsborough County Public Library System.)

This interior views displays one of the hangars at MacDill, dated May 29, 1941. Note the early model B-17. (Courtesy Special Collections, University of South Florida.)

Taken November 13, 1940, this photograph shows the first base commander of MacDill AAFld, General Clarence Tinker, front left. (Courtesy Special Collections, University of South Florida.)

General Tinker is pictured here during a flag raising ceremony at MacDill. This appears to be a formal dedication of the base, which was held on April 15, 1941. (Courtesy St. Petersburg

Historical Society.)

Troops march in review of General Tinker on April 15, 1941. Note the crane barely visible at the far left, indicating that the base was still under construction. (Courtesy Tampa-Hillsborough County Public Library System.)

Civilians inspect early bombers at a MacDill open house event, April 15, 1941. (Courtesy Special Collections, University of South Florida.)

Three
War Comes to Tampa Bay

Merchant seamen practice firing a World War I-vintage Lewis machine gun somewhere near St. Petersburg. (Courtesy St. Petersburg Historical Society.)

An African-American technical sergeant guards a newly arrived B-26 bomber at MacDill. Note the newly completed hangars in the distance. This photograph was taken during the summer of 1943. (Courtesy Special Collections, University of South Florida.)

With the influx of troops, the war boosted the local economy of the bay area. Here, soldiers are patronizing Liggetts Drug Store in Tampa, August 12, 1942. (Courtesy Special Collections, University of South Florida.)

Bars and night clubs began to spring up throughout the area to eagerly welcome the thirsty soldiers and their money. (Courtesy Special Collections, University of South Florida.)

Two Army Air Force officers and an attractive young woman sit at a round table at the Colonnade Restaurant on Bayshore Boulevard in the winter of 1944. This photograph was taken long before the Colonnade became the elegant restaurant it is today. (Courtesy Special Collections, University of South Florida.)

A banquet for the members of the Young Hebrew Association was held in the old German Club in Ybor City on April 18, 1943. The German Club was closed down during the First World War due to the pervasive anti-German sentiment. The club later became the Y.M.H.A. building. (Courtesy Special Collections, University of South Florida.)

Jewish soldiers and sailors attend a banquet held by the Zedek Scharri Synagogue in Tampa, April 19, 1943. (Courtesy Special Collections, University of South Florida.)

Medical officers from MacDill Field attend a banquet at the Tampa Yacht Club, November 24, 1942. (Courtesy Special Collections, University of South Florida.)

A detachment of the Red Cross's Canteen Corps were photographed in Tampa, January 12, 1943. Their goals were to serve as medical assistants and to provide comfort and relief for servicemen far from home. (Courtesy Special Collections, University of South Florida.)

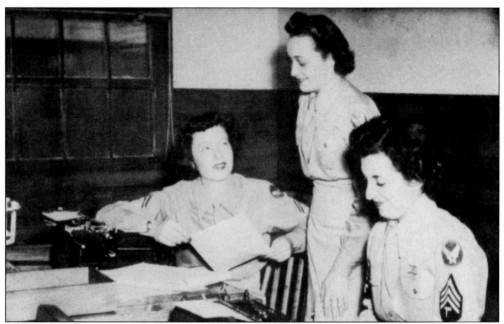

Three members of the Women's Army Corps (WAC) pose in an office at MacDill, winter 1944. MacDill had a considerable number of female civilian employees as well as a strong contingent of WACs throughout the war years. (Courtesy Special Collections, University of South Florida.)

Coast Guardsmen parade down a St. Petersburg street during the war. Scenes such as these were commonplace in many bay area towns on patriotic holidays. (Courtesy St. Petersburg Historical Society.)

During the war, many local businesses were procured by the military in order to meet the wartime demands. Here, army recruits stand in line to receive their meal at the Tramor Cafeteria in downtown St. Petersburg in 1942. Note the canteens carried by the soldiers to ward off dehydration in the harsh Florida sun. (Courtesy St. Petersburg Historical Society.)

The massive influx of men and materials into the bay area was a logistical nightmare for the military. As seen here, army recruits are encamped on the grounds of the Vinoy Park Hotel in 1942, due to the fact that most of St. Petersburg's hotels, converted to barracks use, were already filled to the maximum. These soldiers marched up and down Fourth Street for training. (Courtesy St. Petersburg Historical Society.)

These army recruits were conducting maneuvers somewhere in Pinellas County. Note the obsolete World War I P-17 rifles being used. (Courtesy St. Petersburg Historical Society.)

This was the era of the big bands, and it was only natural for the merchant seamen to have their own. Many military bands played for civilian as well as military audiences. Here, a military band is about to perform on the air with WSUN, a local St. Petersburg radio station. (Courtesy St. Petersburg Historical Society.)

A Civilian Defense information desk is shown at a St. Petersburg bus terminal. The Civilian Defense was created during the war in order to assist military and government agencies in times of war and during disasters. (Courtesy St. Petersburg Historical Society.)

Coast Guardsmen take aim during rifle practice with Springfield Model 1903 rifles. (Courtesy St. Petersburg Historical Society.)

A soldier and his bride were photographed during their marriage ceremony. (Courtesy St. Petersburg Historical Society.)

An aerial shot displays Bayboro Harbor in St. Petersburg. Even though this photograph was taken in 1948, one can clearly see the Coast Guard Air Station (CGAS) and the nearby Maritime Service training station. Note the World War II-era, fleet-type submarine moored along the naval warehouses. (Courtesy Tampa-Hillsborough County Public Library System.)

This image shows a wartime ceremony at the Coast Guard Station at Bayboro Harbor. (Courtesy Tampa-Hillsborough County Public Library System.)

A wartime graduation ceremony of the USMS was held at their Bayboro facility. During World War II, more than 25,000 recruits were trained at the St. Petersburg facility. Note the USMS training ship *American Seaman* in the background. (Courtesy St. Petersburg Historical Society.)

A naval subchaser goes on patrol for German U-boats in the Gulf of Mexico. These boats were stationed at the Bayboro facility. (Courtesy St. Petersburg Historical Society.)

These airmen formed a band known as Jimmie Baker and His Orchestra and are about to perform on the air for WSUN radio. (Courtesy St. Petersburg Historical Society.)

A group photograph of Chinese recruits in St. Petersburg. No other information is known about this group; however, it is interesting to note the one soldier in the back row giving the V for victory sign. (Courtesy St. Petersburg Historical Society.)

Smoke rises from an explosion at Drew Field, August 1942. Was there an enemy attack? No, Hollywood came to town to film the wartime epic film *Air Force* at Drew Field. This is one of the stills from the film. (Courtesy Special Collections, University of South Florida.)

The president of the Tampa Chamber of Commerce, T.G. Mixson (far left), and Secretary Dave Curtis (far right) pose with actor John Garfield (to the right of the sign) during the filming of *Air Force* at Drew Field, August 1942. (Courtesy Special Collections, University of South Florida.)

Another film still from *Air Force* shows a ground crew at work. Many of the extras in the movie were off-duty airmen from MacDill and Drew Fields. (Courtesy Special Collections, University of South Florida.)

A B-17 bomber makes a landing against a dramatic backdrop on the runway at Drew Field during the filming of *Air Force* in August 1942. (Courtesy Special Collections, University of South Florida.)

These Coast Guardsmen of the 7th Platoon posed for this portrait in Tampa, 1944. Note the mast of the *José Gaspar* pirate ship and the Tampa General Hospital on Davis Island in the background. (Courtesy Special Collections, University of South Florida.)

The Tampa Business College provided an education to these army clerks, July 31, 1941. (Courtesy Special Collections, University of South Florida.)

This soldier is posing in front of the landing for a boat service that went between St. Petersburg and MacDill Field. (Courtesy Special Collections, University of South Florida.)

An army private poses in the German prisoner-of-war camp in Drew Field. (Courtesy Special Collections, University of South Florida.)

Though this photograph was taken at Camp Blanding, Florida, it shows the same experiences that German POWs faced when they were interned at Drew Field during the war. German and Italian POWs began arriving at Drew Field in 1942, and many were veterans of Rommel's *Afrika Korps*. (Courtesy National Archives.)

Living conditions for most, if not all, POWs were spartan. Here, Camp Blanding's German POWs are resting from the harsh Florida sun in structures that would have been similarly found at Drew Field. (Courtesy National Archives.)

German and Italian POWs were utilized in agricultural and non-war-related manufacturing purposes. Here, German POWs are collecting citrus from a Florida farm. Another facility near Tampa that handled POWs was located in Dade City. (Courtesy National Archives.)

Four

The Homefront

As war broke out, many able-bodied men who couldn't get into the armed service for one reason or another formed home guard units around the state. One of these was the Florida Defense Force. Pictured here are members of Company B, 5th Battalion in front of their headquarters in Davis Island, June 22, 1942. (Courtesy Special Collections, University of South Florida.)

A group shot possibly shows the same men from Company B, Florida Defense Force; however, their shoulder patches say Home Guard. Rank appeared to be designated by the addition of abbreviated words such as Lt. for Lieutenant and Sgt. for sergeant on the shoulder patches. Note the infantry-style guidon with HG embroidered on it. (Courtesy Special Collections, University of South Florida.)

Tampa native Tommy Gomez is seen here seated with two of his army buddies, March 5, 1942. A well-known prize fighter, at one time Tommy Gomez reached the number three spot in the heavyweight ranks when he was defeated by Jersey Joe Walcott. Gomez achieved a notable military career during the war as well. (Courtesy Special Collections, University of South Florida.)

This female welder was photographed at the Tampa shipyards, September 18, 1943. Because most able-bodied men left their jobs to enlist in the military, women began to take over the vacant positions. During the war, "Rosie the Riveter" became a symbol for these working women. (Courtesy Tampa-Hillsborough County Public Library System.)

Throughout the war, the shipyards at Tampa produced all types of ships for the war effort, from liberty ships to subchasers. Here is the launching of the USS *Mauna Loa* from the Port Tampa berth, April 14, 1943. (Courtesy Tampa-Hillsborough County Public Library System.)

Under construction is the *LT-133* at the Tampa Marine Corporation Shipyard, November 17, 1943. (Courtesy Tampa-Hillsborough County Public Library System.)

The building of Tampa hull #42 is underway at the Tampa Shipbuilding Company, March 1944. When completed, this ship was later named the USS *Sierra*, and it was still in service with the navy as of 1993. The *Sierra* was built as a 10,000-ton destroyer tender. She was assigned to repair duty in the aftermath of Hurricane Andrew. (Courtesy Special Collections, University of South Florida.)

Another view shows the USS *Sierra* at the Tampa shipyards, March 18, 1944. (Courtesy Special Collections, University of South Florida.)

This pre-war aerial view gives us a different look at the Tampa Shipbuilding Company, December 1939. (Courtesy Special Collections, University of South Florida.)

Ships were continuously being built and/or repaired twenty-four hours a day during the war years. This photograph, dated December 6, 1942, shows the Tampa dockyards at full throttle despite blackout restrictions. (Courtesy Special Collections, University of South Florida.)

ARMY-NAVY "E" AWARD
JULY 7, 1944
TAMPA SHIPBUILDING CO., INC

For their war effort, the Tampa Shipbuilding Company received the Army-Navy E award, July 7, 1944. (Courtesy Special Collections, University of South Florida.)

Members of a civilian ground crew, including two women and an old man, work on an aircraft engine at MacDill during the summer of 1943. (Courtesy Special Collections, University of South Florida.)

A scrap drive to gather metal for building wartime equipment was held in front of the Roxy Theatre at 8137 Nebraska Avenue in Sulphur Springs. (Courtesy Special Collections, University of South Florida.)

Another scrap drive was held, this time in Ybor City. Settled in the 1880s by Cuban, Spanish, and Italian immigrants, Ybor City developed, at one time, into the cigar manufacturing capital of the world. Note the scrap sign is in both Spanish and English. (Courtesy Special Collections, University of South Florida.)

The USO Building at 214 North Boulevard was captured on film on February 2, 1942. (Courtesy Tampa-Hillsborough County Public Library System.)

A crowd gathered in the lounge of the USO building, February 28, 1942. (Courtesy Tampa-Hillsborough County Public Library System.)

An unidentified group of Tampa Chapter of the American Red Cross workers are in front of and inside of a mobile canteen vehicle, October 8, 1943. The inscription on the vehicle reads, "Presented to the American Red Cross by the Indiana Grand Chapter, Order of the Eastern Star." (Courtesy Tampa-Hillsborough County Public Library System.)

This group includes women who were employed during the war, as well as some Red Cross workers, April 28, 1943. (Courtesy of Tampa-Hillsborough County Public Library System.)

The same Red Cross vehicle was parked in front of the old Tampa Bay Hotel, which was reutilized as the University of Tampa. (Courtesy Tampa-Hillsborough County Public Library System.)

A patriotic parade of old veterans and Boy Scouts are seen here in the streets of St. Petersburg. Of interest are the different uniforms worn by these veteran groups, such as the United Spanish-War Veterans, American Legion, and British Veterans of the Great War. (Courtesy St. Petersburg Historical Society.)

A scrap drive was conducted by some Boy Scouts in St. Petersburg. (Courtesy St. Petersburg Historical Society.)

A female captain of the Civil Defense was photographed in St. Petersburg during the war. (Courtesy St. Petersburg Historical Society.)

A patriotic storefront window in St. Petersburg shows various military memorabilia, including a World War I-vintage German Maxim 08/15 machine gun. (Courtesy St. Petersburg Historical Society.)

This images reveals a ceremony held by the American Legion and British Veterans of the Great War in St. Petersburg. (Courtesy St. Petersburg Historical Society.)

During wartime in St. Petersburg, mandatory "blackouts" were enforced in order to conceal all lights that might be visible to the enemy during an air raid. Later in the war, blackout restrictions were lessened. (Courtesy St. Petersburg Historical Society.)

A St. Petersburg man is seen here tending to his "Victory Garden." Due to wartime rationing of certain goods and foodstuffs, civilians created small gardens to provide their families with basic vegetables. (Courtesy St. Petersburg Historical Society.)

Three women are eager to help the war effort as volunteers for the Civil Defense in St. Petersburg. (Courtesy St. Petersburg Historical Society.)

A St. Petersburg youngster is praised for her contribution to the war effort. (Courtesy St. Petersburg Historical Society.)

Members of a St. Petersburg American Legion post are seen here collecting records for the troops. (Courtesy St. Petersburg Historical Society.)

Veteran organizations have always been great sources of support when the country is at war. From conducting patriotic rallies to organizing scrap drives, veterans eagerly served their country in the capacity that they could during World War II. Here, American Legionaires present a flag to a pair of army officers. (Courtesy St. Petersburg Historical Society.)

A makeshift recruiting station for the Coast Guard Reserve was located at a street corner on Central Avenue and Fourth Street in St. Petersburg. (Courtesy St. Petersburg Historical Society.)

These two women are examining a war ration coupon book. Practically everything was rationed, from foodstuffs to gasoline. Unnecessary traveling was discouraged. (Courtesy St. Petersburg Historical Society.)

Some volunteers staged this wartime photograph. They are, from left to right: (on the firing line) Private Hampton Forman (instructor) and Captain Jess Taylor; (kneeling) Captain John P. Welch, Private Jack Griffin, Private Enrico Maschino, Corporal Albert Hardy, and Lieutenant Cecil O. Ritch; (standing) Instructor Marshall Johnston, Private Kenneth Stanton, Corporal George Caravasios, Private Cecil O. Ritch Jr., Private First Class Jack Laemmerman, and Sergeant Jack Calkins. Note the diversity of insignia and uniforms of the Civil Air Patrol, Civil Defense, and the Florida Defense Force. (Courtesy St. Petersburg Historical Society.)

Those from the bay area who served overseas never forgot where they came from. This signpost, located somewhere in the Pacific, clearly shows the direction to Ybor City, St. Petersburg, and Tampa. (Courtesy Special Collection, University of South Florida.)

The City of Dunedin put up this honor roll, paying tribute to their townsmen who went off to war. Three hundred and five men from Dunedin served in the war—nine never returned. (Courtesy Dunedin Historical Society.)

Five

One a Day in
Tampa Bay

A B-26 bomber from MacDill trains for low level bombing over Mullet Key during the summer of 1943. (Courtesy Special Collections, University of South Florida.)

A pre-war bomber flies over newly built barracks at MacDill Field. The base became the headquarters for the Third Air Force and was the largest training area for bomber pilots in Florida. (Courtesy A.M. de Quesada.)

African-American engineers at MacDill man a Browning .50 caliber anti-aircraft machine gun during the spring of 1943. During the war, white and black soldiers were placed into segregated units. (Courtesy Special Collections, University of South Florida.)

At MacDill, the army maintained a series of rescue boats for downed aircraft in the bay or in the Gulf of Mexico. During the war, the phrase "One a day in Tampa Bay" was echoed as fifteen B-26 bombers crashed into the bay over a thirty-day period. The boats were completely operated by army rather than by naval personnel! (Courtesy Special Collections, University of South Florida.)

Toward the latter part of the war, Drew Field no longer resembled the cow pasture it once was. With the additional hardstands and a POW complex, Drew became an independent field, though it coordinated military operations with its larger counterpart, MacDill Field. In September 1943, Dale Mabry Highway was opened as a link to the two military installations. (Courtesy National Archives.)

Henderson Army Air Field was an auxiliary field to both Drew and MacDill during the war. Fighters were based here at Henderson. (Courtesy Tampa-Hillsborough County Public Library.)

An aerial view sheds light on Albert Whitted Airport during the war. The navy took possession of the field in 1942 as a facility to train their pilots. Note the number of Stearman and Waco trainers. (Courtesy St. Petersburg Historical Society.)

This aerial view shows Pinellas Army Air Field under construction. Development as a county airport began in March 1941, and the army leased it from Pinellas County in April 1942. (Courtesy St. Petersburg Historical Society.)

During the war, the 304th, 337th, and 440th Fighter Squadrons trained at Pinellas Army Air Field with P-40s and P-51 Mustangs. Earlier, there were Kittyhawks, Aircobras, and Tomahawks that flew from this field. (Courtesy St. Petersburg Historical Society.)

A group photograph shows Army Air Force officers in front of the headquarters building of the 64th Training Wing at Pinellas Army Air Field. (Courtesy St. Petersburg Historical Society.)

A group of Stearman P-17s await a new group of air cadets for training at the Lakeland School of Aeronautics in Lakeland. In July 1942, the facility became the Lodwick School of Aeronautics. Established in 1940 with a staff of civilian and military instructors, the school was to help train army officers to fly in the new Army Air Force. (Courtesy Lakeland Public Library.)

An aerial view of the Lodwick School of Aeronautics complex. Next to the hangars there were five buildings that consisted of two dormitories for 150 cadets, one combination recreation hall/hospital, one combination mess hall/kitchen, and one academic hall for classes. (Courtesy Lakeland Public Library.)

The first Royal Air Force cadets arrived and received their flight training at the Lakeland School in 1941. From 1940 to 1945, the school trained 8,825 men, of which 1,327 were British. (Courtesy Lakeland Public Library.)

The Lakeland School is photographed here under construction in 1940. (Courtesy Lakeland Public Library.)

Army air cadets from the Lodwick School of Aeronautics parade through the streets of Lakeland. Note the distinctive flag made for the school. (Courtesy Lakeland Public Library.)

Air cadets walk in front of a hangar at another training field associated with Albert Lodwick, the Lodwick Aviation Military Academy in Avon Park. (Courtesy A.M. de Quesada.)

Cadets stand at a morning roll call in front of the former Highland Lakes Hotel, which was converted into a barracks for the Lodwick Aviation Military Academy in Avon Park, 1941. After the war the building was turned into a hospital. (Courtesy Lakeland Public Library.)

The Sarasota Army Airfield came into existence in 1942. Two fighter squadrons are operating out of Sarasota, the 98th and the 303rd. Plane count indicated there were fifty-seven P-40s on the base. The Sarasota AAFld was rated as the 337 Fighter Group Fighter Replacement Training Unit. Crews were given two months additional training and then sent off to the war zones. (Courtesy A.M. de Quesada.)

Gunner Students
on 50 Cal. Jeep Range,
Buckingham Army Air Field,
Ft. Myers

PHOTO BY SOUTHEAST ARMY AIR FORCES TRAINING CENTER

Buckingham and Page Army Air Fields were located in Fort Myers during the war. Here, gunner students are seen practicing with their .50 caliber machine guns from the back of trucks. (Courtesy A.M. de Quesada.)

These P-40s are on the ground at Punta Gorda Army Air Field, December 4, 1944. These early war fighters were being used as trainers because the P-38s and P-51s replaced the P-40's status as a combat fighter. (Courtesy A.M. de Quesada.)

This photograph shows a crashed P-40 at the Punta Gorda Army Air Field, February 10, 1945. (Courtesy A.M. de Quesada.)

Six
The Alligator
Goes to War

Donald Roebling (rear row, second from right) poses in front of one of his early creations, the Alligator. These vehicles were initially created as rescue vehicles for hurricane victims, until the navy thought of other potential uses. (Courtesy Dunedin Historical Society.)

This is a close-up view of a Roebling Alligator. (Courtesy Dunedin Historical Society.)

AMPHIBIAN TRACTOR
BOAT REGISTRY NUMBER C-1880
BUILT FOR THE UNITED STATES NAVY
BY DONALD ROEBLING
CLEARWATER, FLORIDA, OCTOBER 1940
BUREAU PLAN № 390556
CAPACITY
BUREAU ENGINE № 11547

This data plate was taken from a Roebling Alligator. Beginning in 1940, Roebling began manufacturing various models of the Alligator for trials conducted by the navy. (Courtesy Dunedin Historical Society.)

Roebling and some of his staff are seen test driving an Alligator for some naval and marine officers on board, 1940. (Courtesy Dunedin Historical Society.)

One of a few variations of the Alligator made for the navy by Roebling, this machine was called the LVT1 Amtrac. Many of the vehicles were manufactured by the Food Machinery Corporation (FMC), with plants in Dunedin and Lakeland. (Courtesy Dunedin Historical Society.)

A later model of the LVT series is seen here at the testing grounds of the Marine Barracks in Dunedin. (Courtesy Dunedin Historical Society.)

War comes to Dunedin. A watchtower was added to the roof of Library Hall. This post was manned by Civil Defense volunteers, who searched the skies for enemy aircraft. At this same time, the old Dunedin Hotel was converted into a U.S. Marine Barracks. (Courtesy Dunedin Historical Society.)

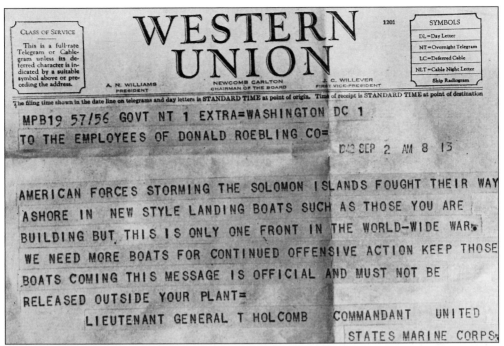

WESTERN UNION

1201

MPB19 57/56 GOVT NT 1 EXTRA=WASHINGTON DC 1

TO THE EMPLOYEES OF DONALD ROEBLING CO=

D42 SEP 2 AM 8 13

AMERICAN FORCES STORMING THE SOLOMON ISLANDS FOUGHT THEIR WAY
ASHORE IN NEW STYLE LANDING BOATS SUCH AS THOSE YOU ARE
BUILDING BUT THIS IS ONLY ONE FRONT IN THE WORLD-WIDE WAR.
WE NEED MORE BOATS FOR CONTINUED OFFENSIVE ACTION KEEP THOSE
BOATS COMING THIS MESSAGE IS OFFICIAL AND MUST NOT BE
RELEASED OUTSIDE YOUR PLANT=
                LIEUTENANT GENERAL T HOLCOMB   COMMANDANT   UNITED
                                                STATES MARINE CORPS.

As the war progressed, the need for more landing crafts in the Pacific campaign were evident, as can be seen in this telegram from Lieutenant General T. Holcomb, USMC. (Courtesy Dunedin Historical Society.)

An aerial view presents the testing grounds of the United States Marine Corps Barracks in Dunedin. This facility was designed to house the marine Alligator operator trainees and their vehicles. (Courtesy Dunedin Historical Society.)

Upon completion of the new Marine Barracks in September 1942, the marines were relocated here from the old Dunedin Hotel. The installation was situated on the southwest corner of Curlew Creek and Alternate 19. (Courtesy Dunedin Historical Society.)

Lieutenant Colonel Maynard M. Nohrden became the commanding officer of the Amphibian Tractor Detachment of the U.S. Marines stationed in Dunedin. He replaced Lieutenant Colonel W.W. Davies when he was assigned to the San Diego Marine Base. (Courtesy Dunedin Historical Society.)

Lt. Col. Nohrden poses with his staff at the Marine Barracks. (Courtesy Dunedin Historical Society.)

Morning flag-raising ceremonies were held at the Marine Barracks. (Courtesy Dunedin Historical Society.)

A LVT is transported through the streets of St. Petersburg by marines. Note the bridge that connected Snell Isle with Coffee Pot Boulevard in the background. (Courtesy St. Petersburg Historical Society.)

A LVT makes a test run off the shore from the training facility of the Marine Barracks in Dunedin. (Courtesy Dunedin Historical Society.)

These marines march through the barracks complex after a ceremony. (Courtesy Dunedin Historical Society.)

LVTs are seen here rolling along in the training grounds of the Marine Barracks. (Courtesy Dunedin Historical Society.)

The citizens of Dunedin, especially the young ladies, made the marines feel at home with numerous parties and dances throughout the war years. (Courtesy Dunedin Historical Society.)

In return, the marines showed their appreciation to the citizens of Dunedin, especially the young ladies. Here, marine NCOs are seen giving aiming tips to these ladies on the training grounds of the Marine Barracks. (Courtesy Dunedin Historical Society.)

Regular exercises included marching from the barracks to Grant Park in Dunedin and back again. Grant Park was later encamped by the 722nd Army Signal Corps AW Company. (Courtesy Dunedin Historical Society.)

Three early LVT1s are seen rolling about on the training fields of the Marine Barracks. This photograph probably dates from about 1941 or 1942. (Courtesy Dunedin Historical Society.)

The marines at the barracks adopted a unit mascot named "Private Screwball," a boxer. Screwball had an official service record, a rating as private, and his own regulation uniform. Traditionally, the USMC permitted only bulldogs to be official mascots. (Courtesy Dunedin Historical Society.)

This LVT1 is on the shores of Dunedin. It appears that concrete blocks are being loaded to possibly test the Amtracs capability of handling heavy weight while in the water. (Courtesy Dunedin Historical Society.)

This photograph shows more testing of a LVT1 in the waters near Dunedin. (Courtesy Dunedin Historical Society.)

A group of LVT1s are seen entering the water from the shore of the Marine Barracks training grounds. (Courtesy Dunedin Historical Society.)

The marines used their LVTs for patriotic rallies and War Bond drives. Here, a LVT is seen in the streets of Dunedin. (Courtesy Special Collections, University of South Florida.)

A Roebling Alligator is placed on display at the old Florida State Fair Grounds, now part of the University of Tampa. (Courtesy Special Collections, University of South Florida.)

A landing craft beached at the Marine Barracks training grounds. On August 4, 1944, the marines shut down their Dunedin base and shipped out. (Courtesy Dunedin Historical Society.)

The success of the Roebling Alligator and the LVT series can be seen in this photograph, for the marines used these vehicles in their island hopping campaigns in the Pacific. (Courtesy Dunedin Historical Society.)

Seven
Aftermath

Soldiers read the news of the ending of the Second World War outside of the offices of the *St. Petersburg Times*. (Courtesy St. Petersburg Historical Society.)

These two navy nurses are holding *St. Petersburg Times* newspapers showing the beginning and the end of the war. (Courtesy St. Petersburg Historical Society.)

The War Assets Administration created a display for the Florida State Fair in 1948. In the years following the war, the War Assets Administration was set up to liquidate all unnecessary surplus produced during the war years. (Courtesy Tampa-Hillsborough County Public Library System.)

These are the Tampa offices of the War Assets Administration, June 30, 1947. (Courtesy Tampa-Hillsborough County Library System.)

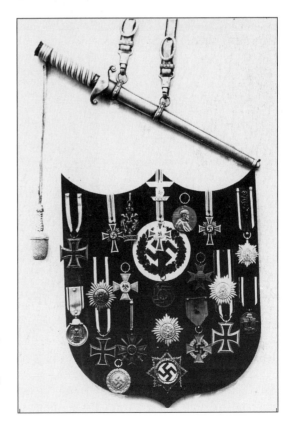

As veterans returned home from the war, they brought with them souvenirs captured from the enemy. Here, we see a German army officer's dagger and various Imperial and Nazi medals. (Courtesy Dunedin Historical Society.)

Sometimes war souvenirs took on a more elaborate form, like this nearly complete dinnerware set of the *Deutsche Reichsbahn*, German Railways. (Courtesy Dunedin Historical Society.)

With the end of war, many military installations reverted back to the local government. Here, we see commercial airlines at the former Pinellas Army Air Field in 1947. Note the barracks in the background. The airport exists today as the St. Petersburg-Clearwater International Airport. (Courtesy St. Petersburg Historical Society.)

On December 18, 1946, Donald Roebling received an award for merit from Admiral Davidson, USN. He also receive a citation signed by President Truman for his role in creating the Alligator. (Courtesy Special Collections, University of South Florida.)

MacDill Field is shown as it looked in 1995. One of the original pre-war hangars is still standing at MacDill Air Force Base. After the war, the air force was created as a separate branch from the army. To this day, MacDill AFB continues to serve Tampa Bay and the nation. (Courtesy A.M. de Quesada.)

This image shows a row of hangars and a pre-war watertower at MacDill AFB. (Courtesy A.M. de Quesada.)

The Art Deco style of the 1930s can clearly be seen on the side of one of the hangars. (Courtesy A.M. de Quesada.)

The prewar watertower can be viewed through the hangar doors. (Courtesy A.M. de Quesada.)

This is the old fire station and guardhouse. (Courtesy A.M. de Quesada.)

This fire hydrant in MacDill AFB is dated 1940, during the time when the base was still under construction. (Courtesy A.M. de Quesada.)

After nearly sixty years of operation, the base theater still actively serves its purpose. (Courtesy A.M. de Quesada.)

The officers' club has changed little since World War II. (Courtesy A.M. de Quesada.)

This landing strip on Mullet Key was meant to be used for aircraft from MacDill and nearby airfields for emergency landings. The site is now Fort DeSoto, a Pinellas County Park. (Courtesy A.M. de Quesada.)

The former United States Maritime Service Training Station buildings in St. Petersburg have been converted into classrooms by the University of South Florida as a school for marine sciences. A monument in front of the main building was dedicated to commemorate the role the USMS Training Station played during the Second World War. (Courtesy A.M. de Quesada.)

Albert Whitted Airport continues to serve as a municipal airport in St. Petersburg. (Courtesy A.M. de Quesada.)

Naval warehouses can still be seen on the way down to the Bayboro Harbor Coast Guard Station. These buildings once catered to the subchaser group stationed here during the war. (Courtesy A.M. de Quesada.)

The Bayboro Harbor Coast Guard Station still continues its duty in the Tampa Bay area. (Courtesy A.M. de Quesada.)

This monument is dedicated to the role that the United States Maritime Service Training Station played during the war. (Courtesy A.M. de Quesada.)

This abandoned runway was once part of Henderson Army Air Field, off of Bougainvillea Avenue. Much of the old field is now part of Busch Gardens, an amusement complex and animal park. (Courtesy A.M. de Quesada.)

Here is a snapshot of an old tiedown from one of Henderson Field's runways, located near the Reynolds Aluminum Plant. (Courtesy A.M. de Quesada.)

A large portion of the runway of Henderson Army Air Field can still be seen behind the Reynolds Aluminum Plant. (Courtesy A.M. de Quesada.)

Hangar Number Three is the only standing structure from the old Pinellas Army Air Field. (Courtesy A.M. de Quesada.)

The interior of Hangar Number Three has changed very little since the war. (Courtesy A.M. de Quesada.)

For a few years, the Florida Military Aviation Museum maintained a collection of WW II aircraft adjacent to the St. Petersburg-Clearwater International Airport. Here, we see a derelict C-47, painted in its WW II paint scheme. The museum shut down in 1996. (Courtesy A.M. de Quesada.)

This 42-foot sponge diving boat was built in 1935 by George Castrinos in Apalachicola, Florida. Originally christened *Apalachicola*, it was used for sponge fishing until the U.S. Navy procured it as an air-sea rescue boat in 1943. After the war, the boat returned to its previous function as a sponge fishing boat until it was decommissioned in 1982. Renamed *Aegean Isles*, it is now on exhibit at the Tarpon Springs Sponge Exchange. (Courtesy A.M. de Quesada.)

Off of Alternate 19 is a small marker showing the site of the Marine Barracks in Dunedin. Nothing remains of the former training facility. (Courtesy A.M. de Quesada.)

This is one of the few army structures remaining at Pass-A-Grille, where the 252nd Coast Artillery were stationed. (Courtesy A.M. de Quesada.)

The former hangars of the Lodwick School of Aeronautics still stand in Lakeland. (Courtesy A.M. de Quesada.)

Here is another view of the hangars and the ramp. These buildings are now maintained by the City of Lakeland Parks and Recreation Department for use as exhibitional or club events. (Courtesy A.M. de Quesada.)

The hangars are the only structures that are left of the old aviation school. (Courtesy A.M. de Quesada.)

The aviation school's runways are now used as roads leading into the complex. (Courtesy A.M. de Quesada.)

Around 1993, the old mess hall of Lodwick Field was torn down to make way for the new general offices of the Detroit Tigers. The baseball team made Lodwick Field its winter home and shares the site with the City of Lakeland. (Courtesy A.M. de Quesada.)

Drane Army Air Field commenced operations in 1942 near Lakeland. After the war, the field became the Lakeland Municipal Airport. Many of the military structures are gone now. Here, a road leads into the foliage at the industrial park adjacent to the airport property. (Courtesy A.M. de Quesada.)

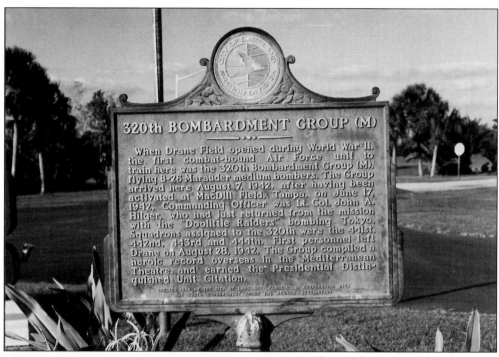

The 320th Bombardment Group Medium trained in Drane Field during the war. In 1980 the City of Lakeland and veterans of the unit erected this historical marker at the present-day airport. (Courtesy A.M. de Quesada.)

Another marker commemorates the 344th Bomb Group Medium that was stationed at Drane Field from December 1942 to January 1944. This was placed at the present-day airport on October 5, 1993, by veterans of the unit. (Courtesy A.M. de Quesada.)

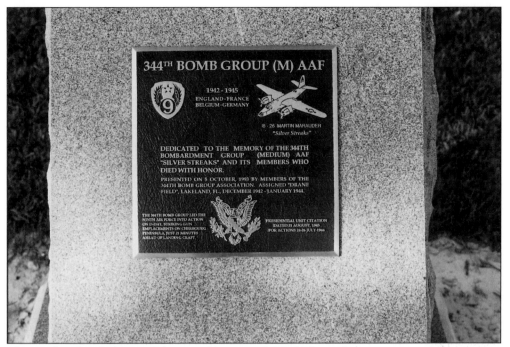

This marker details the unit's history. (Courtesy A.M. de Quesada.)

An old fueling station at Drane Field is overgrown with vines. (Courtesy A.M. de Quesada.)

Relics are still scattered about, reminders of the old military installation's part in the war. Old concrete foundations are now overgrown and forgotten in this wooded area of the industrial park adjacent to the Lakeland Municipal Airport. (Courtesy A.M. de Quesada.)

Fort Dade is shown as it looked in 1983. This was one of five batteries that fortified Egmont Key during the First and Second World Wars. As of 1994, beach erosion has exposed this battery's front portion to the elements, and it may be the next victim to fall into the Gulf of Mexico. (Courtesy A.M. de Quesada.)

In this shot of Fort DeSoto in 1994, we can see what remains of Battery Bigelow. This battery was once armed with two 15-pounder rapid fire guns. During the war, Mullet Key was used as a bombing range for aircraft coming out of MacDill Field. (Courtesy A.M. de Quesada.)

Here is one of the few structures left of the Zephyrhills Army Air Field. This barracks still serves its role as a home for the local air force auxiliary, the Civil Air Patrol. (Courtesy A.M. de Quesada.)

Zephyrhills Army Air Field was home for the 10th Fighter Squadron during the war. This concrete target bunker was used for gunners to sight in their aircraft guns by firing into the structure. The bunker has been converted into a clubhouse by a local skydiving group. (Courtesy A.M. de Quesada.)

Another concrete target bunker is located at the old Brooks Army Air Field near Brooksville. The installation was constructed in 1944 to serve as an auxiliary field for MacDill. It was designed to handle B-17 and B-29 bombers with its three concrete runways, the longest of which was 7,000 feet. This facility received very little military use due to its late construction in WW II, and the site later reverted back to civilian control in 1947. (Courtesy A.M. de Quesada.)

116

These relics were recovered from the old target bunker at Brooks Army Air Field, now known as the Hernando County Airport. (Courtesy A.M. de Quesada.)

One of the only standing structures of the Lodwick Military Aviation Academy is this hangar near Avon Park. (Courtesy A.M. de Quesada.)

Page Army Air Field came into existence when elements of the 98th Bombardment Group arrived in late March 1942. Nearby Buckingham Field was utilized as a gunnery school. (Courtesy A.M. de Quesada.)

The old base chapel still stands in Page Field's industrial area. (Courtesy A.M. de Quesada.)

Both Page and Buckingham Fields returned to civilian control on September 30, 1945. This is one of the old military hangars of Page Field. (Courtesy A.M. de Quesada.)

A marker commemorates the site of Punta Gorda Army Air Field at the Charlotte County Airport. P-40s flew from this field. (Courtesy A.M. de Quesada.)

Another marker remembers the 50th anniversary of the establishment of the Punta Gorda Army Air Field. (Courtesy A.M. de Quesada.)

Only scattered concrete foundations mark where barracks used to be at the Charlotte County Airport. (Courtesy A.M. de Quesada.)

This World War II-era target bunker has been reutilized as a clubhouse for an aviation group at the former Punta Gorda Army Air Field. (Courtesy A.M. de Quesada.)

In Dade City (Pasco County), a historical marker marks the site where a German prisoner-of-war camp was located. The facility was designated Branch Camp Number Seven and consisted of a three-tent mess hall, a canteen with a day room, sleeping quarters, and latrines. Nothing remains of the site, and the property has been turned into a city park. (Courtesy A.M. de Quesada.)

A historical marker commemorates the site of the Venice Army Air Field. The field opened on July 7, 1942, and it was home to P39s, P40s, and P51s. The City of Venice reacquired the facility in 1947. (Courtesy A.M. de Quesada.)

PRESENTED BY
37th & 90th SERV. SQ.'S
27th SERV. GR.
1942 – 1992

A marker near the airport authority office commemorates the units that were stationed at the Venice Army Air Field during the war. (Courtesy A.M. de Quesada.)

Driving around the former military base in Venice, one can notice that some of the streets have retained their original names. (Courtesy A.M. de Quesada.)

In the years following the war, many military buildings were reused for other purposes. This former hangar was used as a storage facility for the Ringling Brothers and Barnum and Bailey Circus. (Courtesy A.M. de Quesada.)

This particular warehouse found use as a business. Note the wartime streetlights. (Courtesy A.M. de Quesada.)

Warehouses and barracks buildings are still found at what was the Venice Army Air Field. (Courtesy A.M. de Quesada.)

This Nissen hut, a rare sight due to its temporary status, still stands after over fifty years at the old Venice Army Air Field. (Courtesy A.M. de Quesada.)

The army returned Drew Field to the City on March 1, 1946. The property became the site of the Tampa International Airport. This photograph was taken in 1991. (Courtesy A.M. de Quesada.)

The two structures at Drew shown in the previous photograph were gone by 1993. Many of the military buildings that made up the old base are rapidly disappearing as the twenty-first century approaches. (Courtesy A.M. de Quesada.)

The Drew Field officers' club is now an apartment complex. (Courtesy A.M. de Quesada.)

Old military warehouses are still scattered about the former base. Many are now homes to local businesses. (Courtesy A.M. de Quesada.)

This wartime hangar, still standing, serves its original purpose. (Courtesy A.M. de Quesada.)

The old base theater at Drew Field still shows movies, though of a different genre. (Courtesy A.M. de Quesada.)

A two-story barracks was preserved by the City of Tampa for use as a recreation center. It is located at 4017 Hesperides Street. (Courtesy A.M. de Quesada.)